Good Old Tunes

Traditional

FOLK HARP
MUSIC of IRELAND

advancing beginner to intermediate

arranged by Susan Call Hutchison

Foreword

Finally! Irish music for the smaller, un-levered harp (C-tuning). Jigs and waltzes, ballads and airs, polkas, even a hornpipe and a sea chanty; all professionally arranged for the harp student.

Arranged on my Harpsicle® 26-string harp, these arrangements can be adapted to even smaller harps, like the 19 string Fireside and the Waring kit harps – just shift the music one octave higher if you need to. And all the melodies (and many of the harmonies) play beautifully even on lap harps and hand-held harps. (Bonus: They sound wonderful on the piano and accordion, too.) I hope you love learning and playing these pieces as much as I enjoyed arranging them for you!

Contents

Introduction

Irish music played on a harp is one of the most beautiful sounds on earth – and maybe even in Heaven. It's surely some of the most fun and satisfying music you can play.

Good Old Tunes is all about helping learning musicians sound the best they can. So, here is a book of beautifully arranged songs specifically for you who are starting your harp journey with a smaller, un-levered harp tuned to a C scale. But that doesn't limit you to the key of C. You'll be playing in C Major, A Minor, D Dorian, etc., and getting that traditional Irish sound.

Fiddlers and other session players often learn these tunes in other keys – but that's for another book. To begin, just enjoy the sound of your harp – or, if they can't resist joining in, ask them to follow along with *your* music. It's very playable!

I wanted this to be an accessible book – suiting the needs of beginners who are just starting to play melody lines as well as players advancing into adding harmony and chords. I arranged it for "26-String" harps – but all of the melodies (and most of the harmonies) can be played on even smaller harps.

BONUS: These arrangements also sound wonderful on piano and accordion or concertina.

Tips for beginning harp players:

- Start with the melody. You will still get a beautiful sound by playing the melody alone.
- In these arrangements, the melody is always the top line of notes.
- Once you are familiar with playing the melody, try adding some harmony!
- Sometimes the harmony is written in the top staff, just under the melody, and sometimes it is all written in in the bottom staff, to be played with the left hand.
- Note: Sometimes the bottom staff will be the treble clef, and sometimes it will be the bass clef. If your harp doesn't play lower notes, you can shift the music up one octave.

Please enjoy your Irish set list as much as I enjoyed creating it for you!

Susan Call Hutchison
Musical Director
Good Old Tunes Publications

Good Old Tunes
Rue and Thyme

Traditional Irish Folk Ballad
arranged by Susan Call Hutchison

Andante

Good Old Tunes
Londonderry Air

Traditional Irish Air
arranged by Susan Call Hutchison

Good Old Tunes
Molly Malone

Traditional Irish ballad
arranged by Susan Call Hutchison

Andante

The Star of the County Down

Traditional Irish Tune
arranged by Susan Call Hutchison

Good Old Tunes
The South Wind

17th Century Irish
arranged by Susan Call Hutchison

2

Good Old Tunes

Captain O'Kane

Turlough O'Carolan
arranged by Susan Call Hutchison

Andante

13

Good Old Tunes

Blind Mary

Turlough O'Carolan
arranged by Susan Call Hutchison

Andante

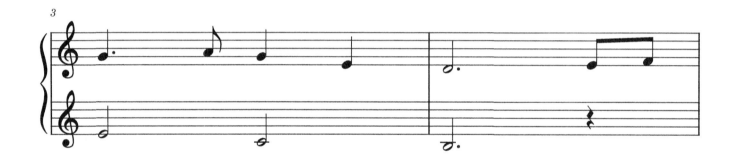

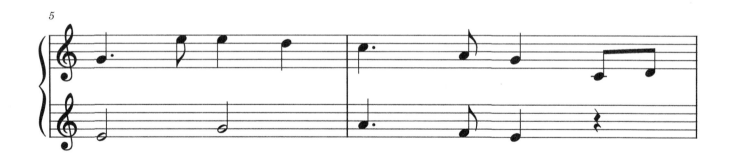

2

Good Old Tunes
The Road to Lisdoonvarna

Traditional Irish Jig
arranged by Susan Call Hutchison

As lively as you like

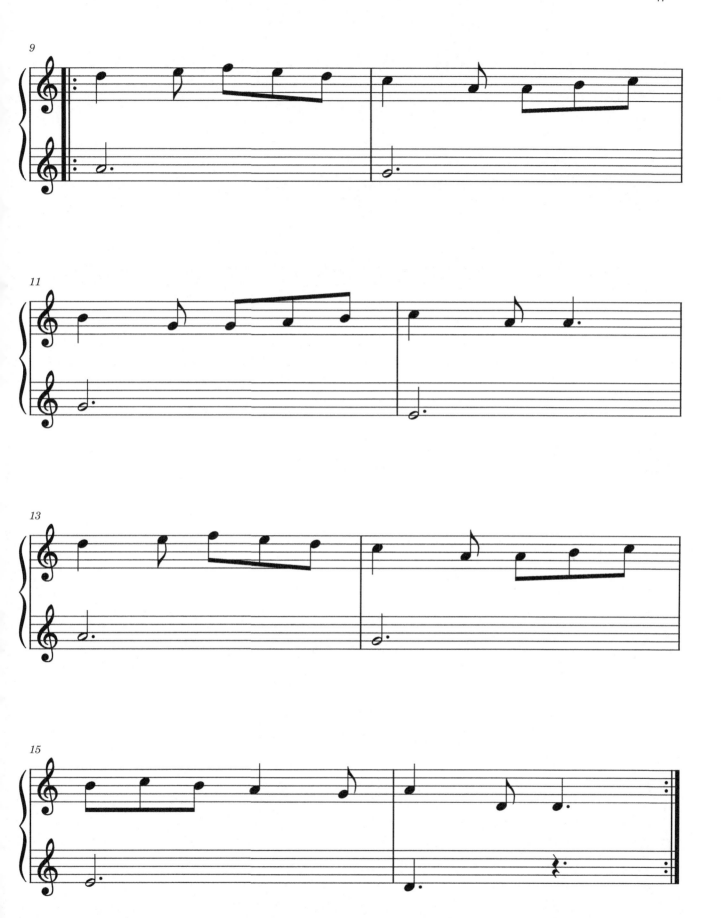

Good Old Tunes

I Love Thee No More

Traditional Irish
arranged by Susan Call Hutchison

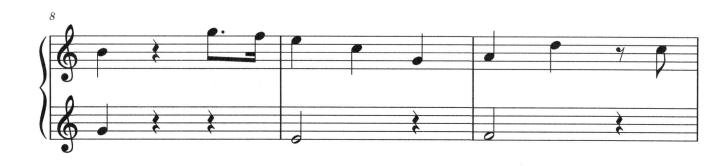

Good Old Tunes

The Lilting Banshee

Traditional Irish Jig
arranged by Susan Call Hutchison

As fast or as slow as you like

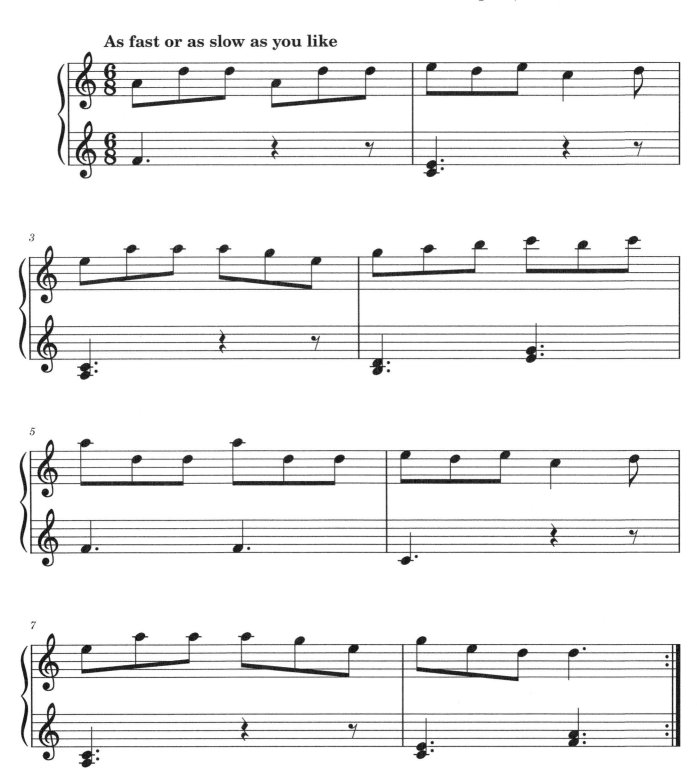

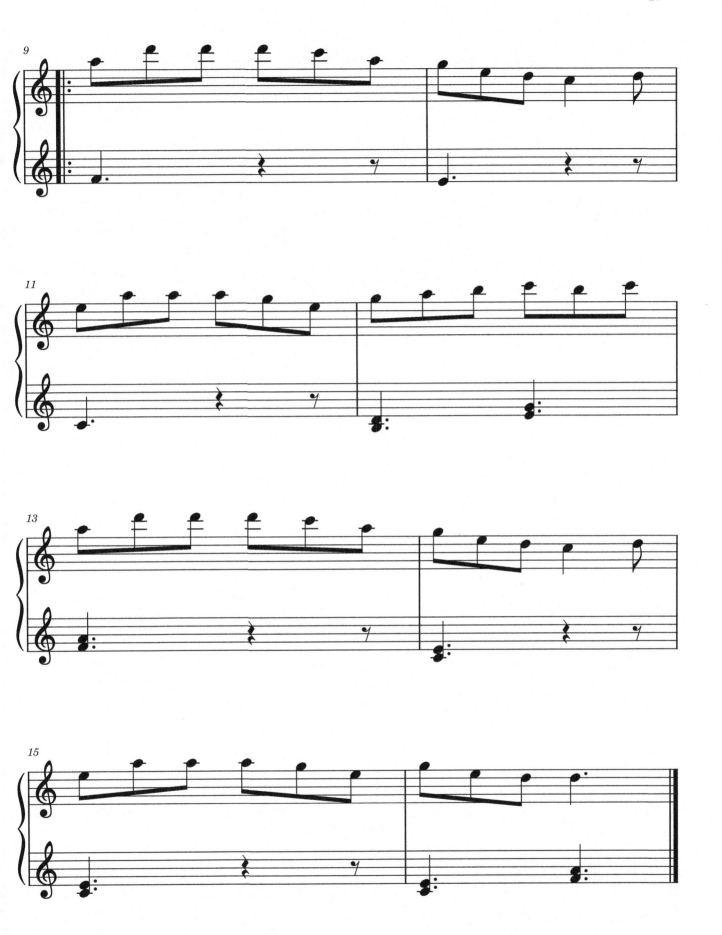

Good Old Tunes

The Rakes of Mallo

Traditional Irish Polka
arranged by Susan Call Hutchison

As a lively polka

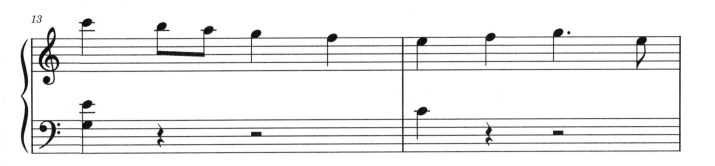

Good Old Tunes

My Own Heart's Delight

Traditional Irish
arranged by Susan Call Hutchison

Andante

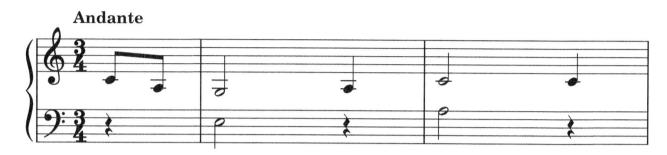

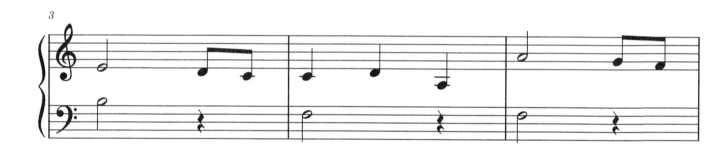

Good Old Tunes

Off to Sea Once More

Traditional Sea Chanty
arranged by Susan Call Hutchison

Allegro

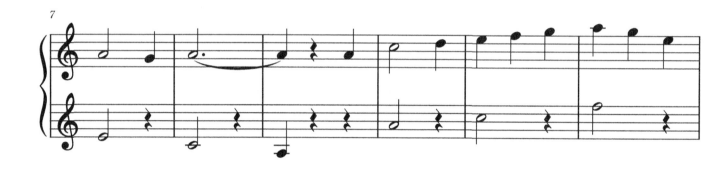

Good Old Tunes

The Minstrel Boy

Irish Folk Song
arranged by Susan Call Hutchison

Good Old Tunes

Swallowtail Jig

Traditional Irish Jig

arranged by Susan Call Hutchison

As lively as you like

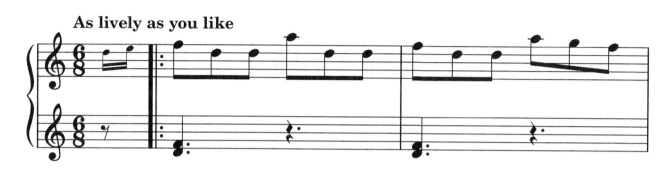

Good Old Tunes

My Darling Asleep

Traditional Irish tune
arranged by Susan Call Hutchison

Good Old Tunes
The Piper's Wife

Traditional Irish
arranged by Susan Call Hutchison

As a lilting waltz

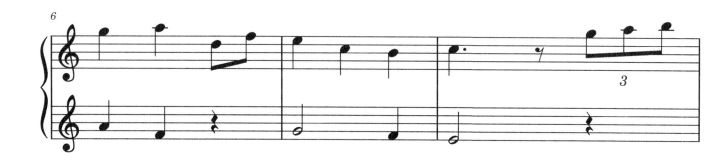

Down by the Sally Gardens

Traditional Irish Air
arranged by Susan Call Hutchison

Good Old Tunes

The Boys of Bluehill

Traditional Irish Hornpipe
arranged by Susan Call Hutchison

Printed in Great Britain
by Amazon

46502971R00024